Arctic Foxes
of the Tundra

By Joyce Jeffries

KidHaven
PUBLISHING

Published in 2018 by
KidHaven Publishing, an Imprint of Greenhaven Publishing, LLC
353 3rd Avenue
Suite 255
New York, NY 10010

Designer: Deanna Paternostro
Editor: Vanessa Oswald

Photo credits: Cover Josef Pittner/Shutterstock.com; p. 5 NaturesMomentsuk/Shutterstock.com; p. 7 Eugene Kalenkovich/Shutterstock.com; p. 9 Ignatiev Alexandr/Shutterstock.com; p. 11 Bildagentur Zoonar GmbH/Shutterstock.com; p. 13 bikeriderlondon/Shutterstock.com; p. 15 Warren Metcalf/Shutterstock.com; p. 17 Andrew Astbury/Shutterstock.com; p. 19 Steven Kazlowski/Getty Images; p. 21 (top), back cover Mario7/Shutterstock.com; p. 21 (bottom) Nagel Photography/Shutterstock.com.

Cataloging-in-Publication Data

Names: Jeffries, Joyce.
Title: Arctic foxes of the tundra / Joyce Jeffries.
Description: New York : KidHaven Publishing, 2018. | Series: Animals of the tundra | Includes index.
Identifiers: ISBN 9781534522275 (pbk.) | 9781534522244 (library bound) | ISBN 9781534522176 (6 pack) | ISBN 9781534522206 (ebook)
Subjects: LCSH: Arctic fox–Juvenile literature.
Classification: LCC QL737.C22 J43 2018 | DDC 599.776'4–dc23
Printed in the United States of America

CPSIA compliance information: Batch #BS17KL: For further information contact Greenhaven Publishing LLC, New York, New York at 1-844-317-7404.

Please visit our website, www.greenhavenpublishing.com. For a free color catalog of all our high-quality books, call toll free 1-844-317-7404 or fax 1-844-317-7405.

Contents

Living in the Tundra

Arctic foxes live in the tundra and mountains, mainly near the Arctic Ocean. The tundra is a flat, treeless place with frozen ground. This **habitat** is very cold, but these animals have **adapted** to this place and call it home.

How do arctic foxes build their homes? Read on to find out!

Arctic foxes live in **dens**.
They build these homes by
burrowing into cliffs and under
the ground. To avoid the chilly
tundra winds, they dig deep
into the snow and hide.

Arctic foxes are also
called white foxes
or polar foxes.

Arctic foxes' furry coats warm their bodies in low temperatures. They have many **layers** of fur, including a white or blue-gray outer layer. These colors help them blend in with the snow.

Arctic foxes can survive
in temperatures as low
as –58 degrees Fahrenheit
(–50 degrees Celsius).

winter coat

Arctic foxes **shed** their outer layers of fur in the spring and become gray or brown. They appear **camouflaged** against the tundra's rocks and plants. In the winter, they grow their white fur back.

Arctic foxes can blend in with their surroundings, which makes it easy for them to hide from **predators**.

summer coat

11

Staying Warm in the Cold

The small body parts of arctic foxes, such as their small ears and short nose, help keep body heat in. They also have furry paws that help them stay warm the cold.

An arctic fox's body is built for life in the tundra.

small ears

short nose

13

An arctic fox's bushy tail is called a "brush." The fox stays warm by wrapping its thick brush around itself when spending time out in the cold and windy weather.

An arctic fox's brush keeps it warm and helps with its balance, too!

brush

15

Searching for Food

Arctic foxes are omnivores, which means they eat both meat and plants. Foods they often eat include **lemmings**, birds, fish, and berries. To prepare for the winter, arctic foxes store food.

Arctic foxes have a strong sense of hearing, which helps them hear their **prey** when hunting for food.

Another way an arctic fox finds food is by following polar bears that are hunting. Once a polar bear has killed its prey, the arctic fox eats the leftover meat.

Arctic foxes have to be careful not to get eaten by polar bears while following these large predators around!

Fox Families

After arctic foxes **mate** in the spring, the mother arctic fox can have up to 14 pups. Fox families, which include the mother, father, and pups, only live together for a few months.

Learning More

How tall is an arctic fox?	up to 12 inches (30 cm) at the shoulder
How long is an arctic fox?	up to 27 inches (69 cm) from head to rear; tail is up to 14 inches (36 cm)
How much does an arctic fox weigh?	about 17 pounds (8 kg)
How long does an arctic fox live?	about six years in the wild
What does an arctic fox eat?	some plants; animals, such as lemmings, birds, and fish; and dead animals

Arctic foxes are cute, furry creatures!

Glossary

adapt: To change to live better in a certain environment.

burrow: To dig a hole or tunnel to turn it into a living space.

camouflage: To blend in with the surroundings because of certain colors and shapes on an animal's body.

den: A living space built by digging holes and tunnels into the sides of cliffs or underground.

habitat: The natural area where an animal lives.

layer: A part of something lying over or under another part.

lemming: An animal with a small, thick, furry body that lives in northern areas.

mate: To come together to make babies.

predator: An animal that hunts other animals for food.

prey: An animal hunted by other animals for food.

shed: To lose fur or hair.

For More Information

Websites

National Wildlife Federation: Arctic Foxes

www.nwf.org/Kids/Ranger-Rick/Animals/Mammals/Arctic-Foxes.aspx
This website includes fun facts about arctic foxes.

San Diego Zoo: Arctic Fox

kids.sandiegozoo.org/animals/mammals/arctic-fox
The San Diego Zoo provides interesting information on arctic foxes.

Books

Franchino, Vicky. *Arctic Foxes*. New York, NY: Children's Press, 2014.

Murray, Julie. *Arctic Foxes*. Minneapolis, MN: ABDO Publishing Company, 2014.

Index